D1317847

MAKING GOOD CHOICES
A BOOK ABOUT RIGHT AND WRONG

Written by

Lisa O. Engelhardt

Illustrated by

Anne FitzGerald

ABBEY PRESS
Publications
St. Meinrad, IN 47577

Text © 2012 Lisa O. Engelhardt
Illustrations © 2012 St. Meinrad Archabbey
Published by Abbey Press Publications
1 Hill Drive
St. Meinrad, Indiana 47577

All rights reserved.
No part of this book may be used or reproduced in any manner
without written permission of the publisher, except in the case of
brief quotations embodied in critical articles and reviews.

Library of Congress Catalog Number
2012949176

ISBN 978-0-87029-514-0

Printed in the United States of America.

A Message from the Author to Parents and Caring Adults

Learning to do right is a lifelong endeavor, as we all know only too well. Since children are relative newcomers on the path of social, moral, and spiritual development, they especially need caring guides to teach them right and wrong. Parents, teachers, and caring adults are their preeminent mentors and role models.

One of the primary ways to teach children right from wrong is to establish rules and consistently enforce them. We can reward good actions with appropriate praise or a tangible reward like a sticker or special privilege. Poor decisions may result in a time out, having a card pulled in the classroom, or a privilege withdrawn.

Even very young children can learn that every action has broader consequences. Point out to children how wrong choices affect themselves and others: "Hitting your little sister makes her cry. How would you feel if someone bigger hit you?" Conversely, we can show how doing good *feels* good and is its own reward. If you help an elderly woman with her groceries, for instance, you and your child will experience the positive reinforcement of her smile and gratitude.

Everyday experiences provide great moral learning opportunities. After a worship service, talk about the readings and sermon to help your child understand them. As you read books together, talk about the good and bad implications of the characters' actions. After you see a movie, discuss the conflict in the film—why it happened, what effects it had, how it was resolved.

Most importantly, we must practice what we preach. If your child sees you tell a "little white lie," for example, then she is going to learn this behavior. On the other hand, if you deliver a casserole to a bereaved neighbor, your child will see you doing good and will want to emulate this.

When we show children how to be compassionate, empathetic, and caring, not only are we teaching them about right and wrong, but we are helping to mold them into loving, responsible people. And, in doing so, we are making the world a kinder, gentler place—child by child by child.

—*Lisa O. Engelhardt*

You have a secret power!

You have the power to choose right or wrong.

Doing what's right means doing what is good for you and good for others. It means being fair, helpful, kind, and loving.

Doing wrong means hurting other people or messing up their stuff.

Playing by the rules.

Your parents have been teaching you about right and wrong since you were very little. Your teachers, coaches, and church leaders also teach you about it.

When you act in the right way, you are able to learn better, play better, and be a better person.

Use the "Golden Rule."

At church or in school, you may have learned about the "Golden Rule": Treat others the way you would like them to treat you.

Before you do something, think: How would I feel if someone did this to me?

We are the world.

You can also think about: What if everybody in the world did this thing? What would happen?

What if everybody in the world threw their empty cans on the ground instead of in the garbage? Pretty soon there would be trash all over!

What would your hero do?

Do you know someone who is always very good and kind? Maybe your grandma, your teacher, or someone you learned about at church or in a book?

When you're trying to pick the right thing to do, ask yourself: What would my hero do?

Just say no.

Sometimes your friends might want to do something that you know is wrong.

Try to suggest something else to do.

If your friends won't listen, then just say, "I don't want to do this. You can count me out." And walk away.

Getting away with it.

You may do something wrong, but nobody finds out. Just because you don't get caught doesn't mean it's okay.

You may have a bad feeling about it. Deep in your heart, you know it was wrong.

Make up for your mistakes.

If you do a bad thing, try to make it better.
Tell the person you hurt that you are sorry.

If you messed up someone's stuff, see if you
can fix it, or buy a new one with
your own money.

Forgiveness.

To forgive someone means to stop being mad at them.

Sometimes we need to forgive other people. Sometimes we need to ask them to forgive us.

If it's really hard to forgive someone, God will help you. Just ask!

Trying to do good counts.

What if you are trying to do the right thing, but something goes wrong?

Even if the other person is sad or mad at the moment, they will know you were trying to help out.

If you're getting hurt...

If someone is hurting you, ask that person to "Please stop!" Or just walk away. If that person won't stop hurting you, tell a grown-up.

Do not hurt someone who hurt you. That just keeps the meanness going.

Feeling and acting.

Just because you *feel* mad doesn't mean you have to *act* bad.

Say a little prayer and ask God to help you calm down. Or do something that takes a lot of energy but doesn't hurt anybody.

Practice makes perfect.

The more you try to do right, the better you will get. It takes practice, like playing a sport or the piano.

You will find that doing good makes others feel good, and that makes YOU feel good!

YOU can be a hero!

You can do good things just for fun, even if
no one knows.

You will be a Do-Good Superhero, using your
secret power to make the world a better place.

Do what is kind, caring, and loving—
and you will always do right.

Lisa O. Engelhardt is the retired editorial director for Abbey Press and a freelance greeting card and giftware writer. The author of 13 children's and gift books, she specializes in inspirational and religious writing. She loves reading novels, taking walks, and being in water. She is endlessly inspired by children and nature.

Anne FitzGerald is an internationally known artist and has written and illustrated over 200 children's books. She is creator of "Dear God Kids" and many other children's books and products. Anne works from her studio/gallery in Limerick, Ireland, and teaches art in Liberty Christian School there.

For other books in this series go to:
www.abbeypresspublications.com
and click on "JUST FOR ME BOOKS" in the side bar.